YOUR KNOWLEDGE HAS VALUE

Ronny Müller

3 Assignments about Phonological Processes

GRIN Verlag

Bibliografische Information der Deutschen Nationalbibliothek:

Die Deutsche Bibliothek verzeichnet diese Publikation in der Deutschen National-
bibliografie; detaillierte bibliografische Daten sind im Internet über http://dnb.d-
nb.de/ abrufbar.

Imprint:

Copyright © 2012 GRIN Verlag GmbH
Druck und Bindung: Books on Demand GmbH, Norderstedt Germany
ISBN: 978-3-656-35434-5

This book at GRIN:

http://www.grin.com/en/e-book/205458/3-assignments-about-phonological-processes

GRIN - Your knowledge has value

Der GRIN Verlag publiziert seit 1998 wissenschaftliche Arbeiten von Studenten, Hochschullehrern und anderen Akademikern als eBook und gedrucktes Buch. Die Verlagswebsite www.grin.com ist die ideale Plattform zur Veröffentlichung von Hausarbeiten, Abschlussarbeiten, wissenschaftlichen Aufsätzen, Dissertationen und Fachbüchern.

Visit us on the internet:

http://www.grin.com/

http://www.facebook.com/grincom

http://www.twitter.com/grin_com

-Universität Erfurt-

PHONOLOGICAL PROCESSES

Wintersemester 2011/12

Homework 1-3

Ronny Müller

Bachelor Geschichtswissenschaft, Anglistik

3. Fachsemester

Homework 1: orchestration

You're so sweet to have done this.

[jʊɹ soʷ swi:tʰu: hæv dʌ̃n ðɪs]

A spoken utterance is phonetically transcribed with a separate column for each speech segment in an orchestration. There are tiers drawn for each different articulator showing their state or location in the production of the utterance. So orchestration is useful to figure out what is going on with the different articulators in the production of the (fluent) speech. Also it is useful to find out how and why certain synchronous "phonological processes" occur. There are five different tiers shown in an orchestration. On the one hand there are tiers for the position of lips, tongue apex and tongue dorsum and on the other hand there are tiers for state of the velum and state of the vocal folds.

Orchestration:

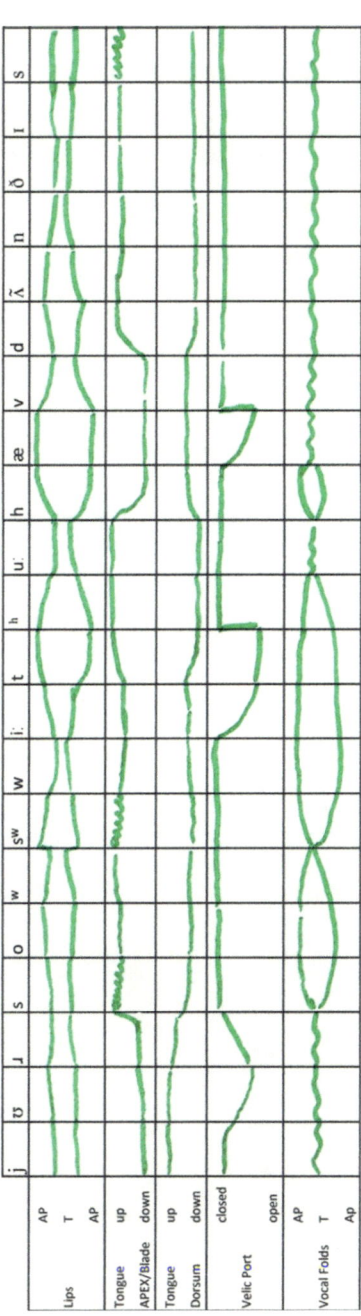

Lips: The lips are mostly together at the beginning, moving a bit apart by producing the [ʊ] and the [o] sound. By producing the [sʷ] sound the lips are more apart. We can see that the lips are mostly apart by speaking the [tʰ] and the [æ] sound.

Tongue: The tongue apex as you can see is moving through the sentence from a lower position to an upper position while producing sounds with turbulence ([s]) indicated in the orchestration with swirls. The tip of the tongue is up while producing [hæv]. The tongue dorsum is mostly down moving through the sentence.

Velic port: The velic port is mostly closed during the sentence.

Vocal Folds: Moving through the sentence they are apart in [soʷ] and [swi:tʰ] and [h].

Homework 2: spectrogram analysis – English words

Analyzing the spectrogram:

Firstly I recorded myself pronouncing the two words "cat" and "fight" with the program PRAAT. The results of recording these two words are shown in the two following spectrograms. I generated them with PRAAT too. The first spectrogram shows the word "cat" and the second spectrogram shows the word "fight".

1) "cat"

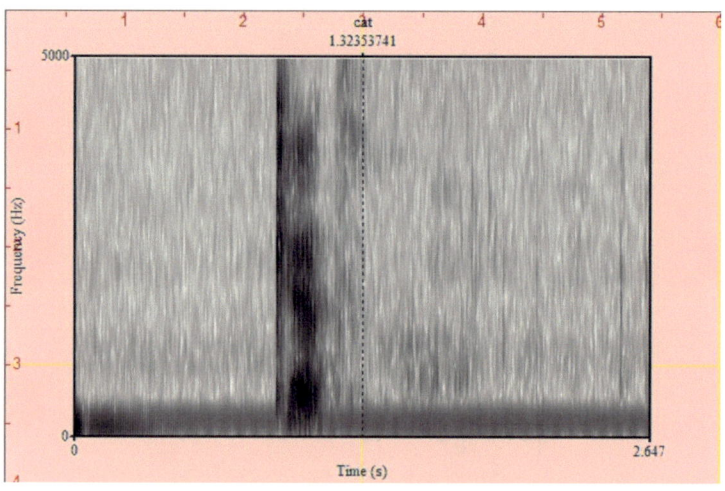

2) "fight"

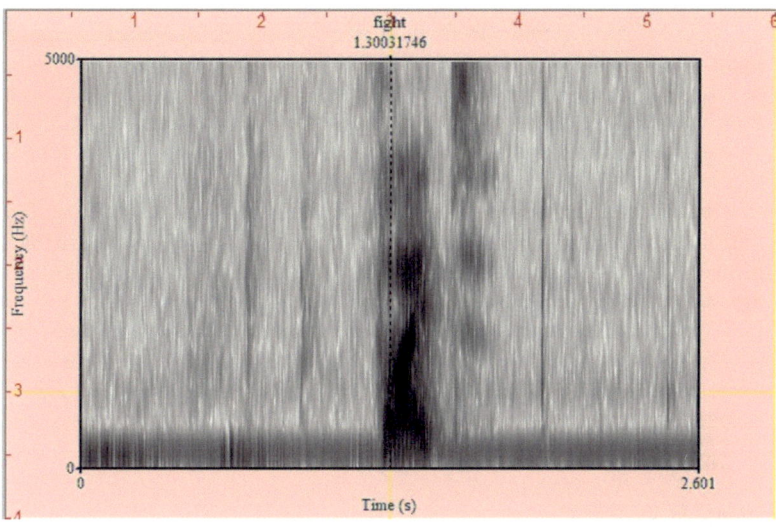

The next step was dividing those two spectrograms into segments.

1) [kʰæ t]

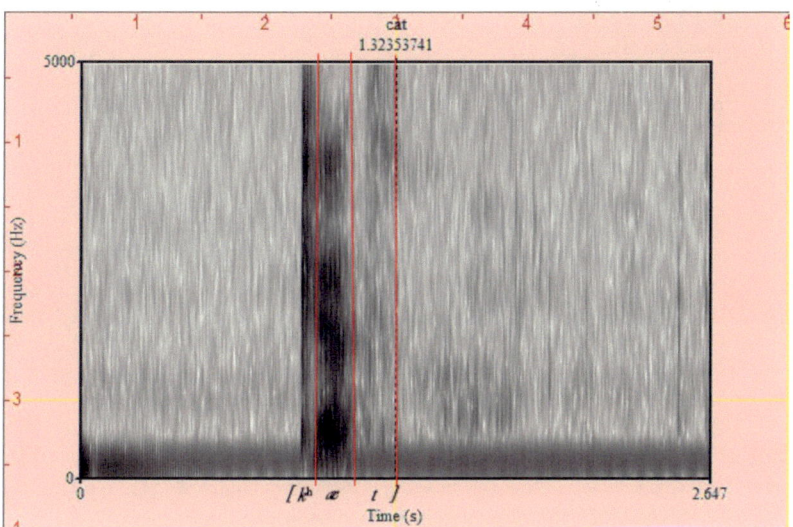

The "cat" spectrogram shows from 0,92 seconds to 0,98 seconds the first consonant segment. This segment represents the plosive voiceless aspirated [kʰ]. We can see the segment is a voiceless aspirated stop because there is a small period of aspiration shown in the spectrogram. The following segment starts from 0,98 seconds to 1,15 seconds. We can see the segment is a vowel because there are clear striations, showing voicing. The vowel is a near open front vowel. The segment has strong amplitude, as seen by the acoustic energy throughout the segment which is shown by the darkness of the striations. As well the segment has a clear formant structure: F1, F2 and F3 frequencies are visible. F1 has a frequency about 540 Hz, which points to the vowel being a high vowel, as F1 is inversely proportional to vowel height. F2 has a high formant value which is about 1800 Hz, which points to the vowel being a front vowel as F2 directly proportional to vowel frontness and backness. F3 has a frequency about 2300 Hz and shows that the vowel is unrounded because F3 is not pointing downwards (related to F2 values). The last segment begins at 1, 15 seconds and ends at 1, 34 seconds. The last segment represents the unvoiced, plosive alveolar element in the spectrogram. It's depending on the frequency of the noise of the burst which is for alveolar sounds above 2300 Hz.

2) [faɪt]

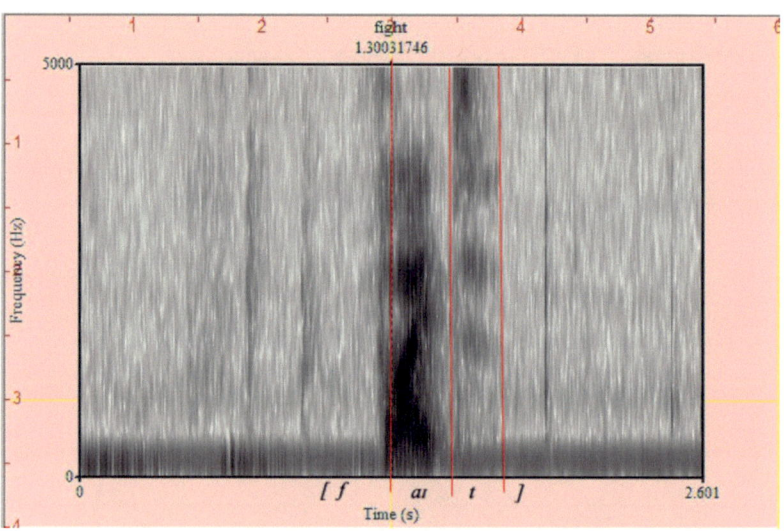

The "fight" spectrogram shows from 1, 23 seconds to 1, 27 seconds the first consonant segment. This segment represents the unvoiced fricative labiodentals [f]. We can see the segment is a voiceless fricative because there is a band of high-frequency, high-intensity energy and a rapid loss at lower frequencies. There are no regular striations, no voice bar, but rather random noise patterns, especially in higher frequency regions. The following segment starts from 1, 27 seconds to 1, 55 seconds. We can see the segment is a diphthong [aɪ] because they are shown clearly in formant plots, as are glides. The two spectral targets can be seen in the formants and the formants show a movement. The formants are particularly long and in general a long, moving formant is proof for a diphthong. F1 has a frequency about 750 Hz, followed by F2 frequency at about 1250 Hz. F3 frequency is about 2470 Hz. The last segment represents the unvoiced, plosive alveolar element in the spectrogram like in the "cat" spectrogram. It's also depending on the frequency of the noise of the burst which is for alveolar sounds above 2300 Hz as seen in the spectrogram.

The consonant sounds in the words are voiceless because the striations throughout the frequency range are irregular/ random. This means the sounds are voiceless. If they would have regular and clear striations, the sounds would be voiced.

æ   aɪ

The following is a comparison between the vowel sound in "cat" and the diphthong in "fight". They are nearly identical at the first view. One difference between them is the distance between F1 and F2 frequencies. The [æ] has F1 frequency about 540 Hz and the [aɪ] has one about 750 Hz. F2 is in [æ] 1800 Hz and in [aɪ] 1250 Hz. [æ] has a F3 frequency about 2300 Hz and [aɪ] has one about 2470 Hz which is approximately the same. The gap in [æ] is about 1260 Hz and the gap in [aɪ] is about 1550 Hz. In general the diphthong [aɪ] has higher frequencies as the vowel [æ]. This means you have to be very specific by looking at it more closely. They also differ in their length. ([aɪ] = 0, 28 s [æ] = 0,17s) Generalized they both have nearly the same appearance for the spectator, but they differ in details.

Homework 3: spectrogram analysis – German words

Analyzing the spectrogram:

Firstly I recorded myself pronouncing the two words "Sohn" and "Haus" with the program PRAAT. The results of recording these two words are shown in the two following spectrograms. I generated them with PRAAT too. The first spectrogram shows the word "Sohn" and the second spectrogram shows the word "Haus".

1) "Sohn"

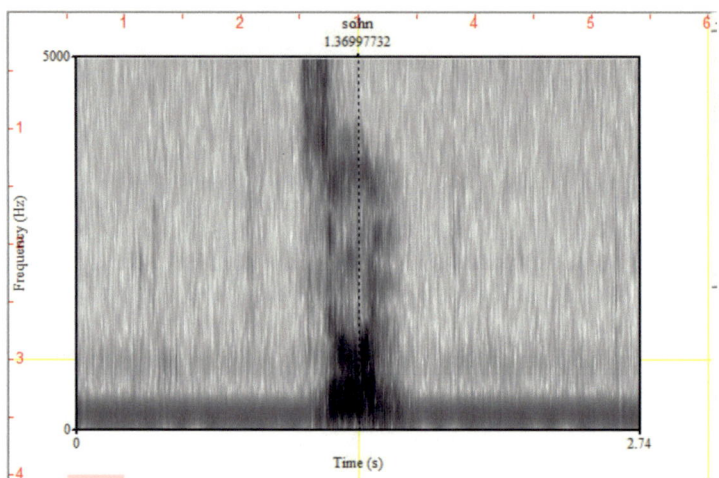

2) "Haus"

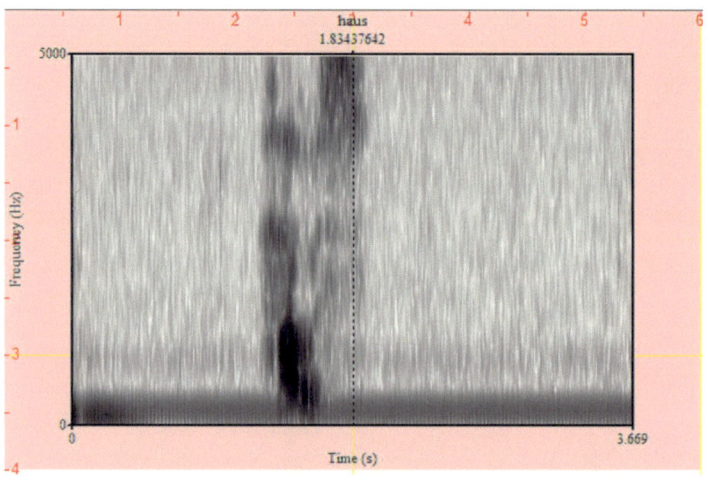

The next step was dividing those two spectrograms into segments.

1) [zo:n]

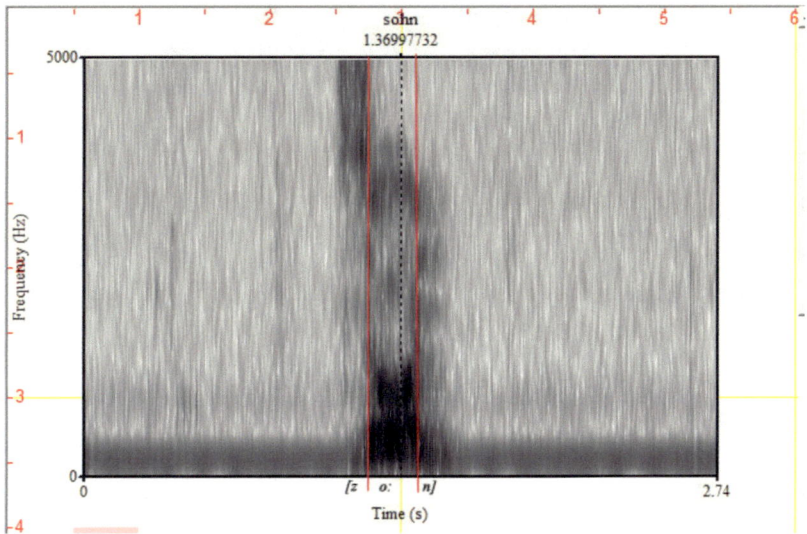

The "Sohn" spectrogram shows from 1, 08 seconds to 1, 23 seconds the first consonant segment. This segment represents the voiced fricative alveolar [z]. Characterizing for this consonant are vertical striations indicating voicing, but only a few can be seen in general. The voiced fricatives are characterized by less intensity and especially for an alveolar place of articulation and there is a frequency burst above 2300 Hz. The following segment starts from 1, 23 seconds to 1, 45 seconds. We can see the segment is a long vowel because there are clear striations, showing voicing. The vowel is a close mid back vowel. The segment has strong amplitude up to a frequency range of 1400 Hz. The acoustic energy throughout the segment is shown by the darkness of the striations. As well the segment has a clear formant structure: F1 and F2 frequencies are clearly visible. F3 frequency shows some kind of vagueness. F1 has a frequency about 450 Hz, which points to the vowel being a high vowel, as F1 is inversely proportional to vowel height. F2 has a lower formant value which is about 1100 Hz, which points to the vowel being a back vowel as F2 directly proportional to vowel frontness and backness. F3 is very faint and has a frequency about 3400 Hz and shows that the vowel is rounded because there is a lowering of the F3 value. The last segment begins at 1, 45 seconds and ends at 1, 57 seconds. The last segment represents the voiced, nasal and bilabial element in the spectrogram. It's depending on a broad peak of low-frequency energy. Voice bar and regular striations are characterized by a medium intensity.

2) [haʊs]

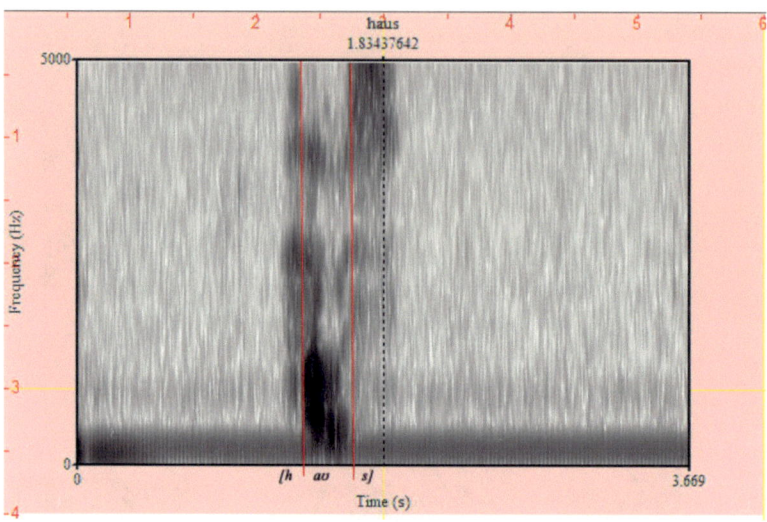

The "Haus" spectrogram shows from 1, 23 seconds to 1, 34 seconds the first consonant segment. This segment represents the unvoiced fricative glottal [h] sound. We can see the segment is a voiceless fricative because there is a band of high-frequency, high-intensity energy and a rapid loss at lower frequencies. There are no regular striations, no voice bar, but rather random noise patterns, especially in higher frequency regions. The following segment starts from 1, 34 seconds to 1, 62 seconds. We can see the segment is a diphthong [aʊ] because it is shown clearly in formant plots. The two spectral targets can be seen in the formants and the formants show a movement. The formants are particularly long and in general a long, moving formant is proof for a diphthong. F1 has a frequency about 450 Hz, followed by F2 frequency at about 1060 Hz. F3 frequency is faint and about 3800 Hz. The last segment represents the unvoiced, fricative alveolar element in the spectrogram. There is a band of high frequency, high intensity energy and there is rapid energy attenuation at lower frequencies. The major energy occurs above 3000 Hz. Also characterizing is the frequency of the noise of the burst which is for alveolar sounds above 2300 Hz as seen in the spectrogram.

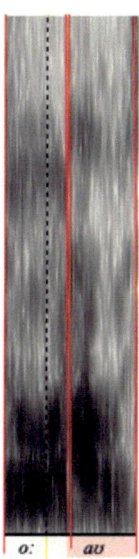

o: aʊ

The following is a comparison between the vowel sound in "Sohn" and the diphthong in "Haus". They are nearly identical at the first view. They both show characteristic features like clear striations and strong amplitude and they both have a clear formant structure. Only by looking at them more closely differences can be found in frequencies. They also differ in their length. ([oː] = 0, 22s [aʊ] = 0, 28s) Generalized they both have nearly the same appearance for the spectator, but they differ in details like F1, F2 and F3 frequencies and especially in their length.

sʃ   [z

The following is a comparison between the voiced fricative segment of "Sohn" with the voiceless fricative segment at the same place of articulation of the second word "Haus". They look nearly identical and no big differences are visible in the spectrogram. I did not expect big differences because both sounds are very similar to each other. The only difference is that the [z] is voiced and the [s] is voiceless. In general a voiced sound can be identified through regular and clear striations while voiceless sounds can be identified through an irregular/random frequency range. Voiced fricatives are characterized by less intensity (they seem fainter) than their voiceless counterparts.